MW01620860

# Short & Tall Tales of Hilton Head Island

Text by Margaret Greer
Photographs by Barry Lowes

Front Cover:
Photograph of
the Harbour Town Lighthouse
is used with permission from
Sea Pines Company, Inc.

Back Cover:
Dolphin Head, Hilton Head Plantation

SPECIAL APPRECIATION TO
*My husband, Walter Greer,*
*For the use of his sketchbooks,*
*Reproductions of his oil paintings,*
*Old photographs,*
*And*
*Most of all for his continual encouragement.*

DESIGN: KAYE BLACK
KAREN BURKY
IAN SKELTON
OF CURRY PRINTING
HILTON HEAD ISLAND, SC

ISBN 0-9761618-053400

PRINTED IN
ALTONA, MANITOBA, CANADA
BY D.W. FRIESEN

# Preface

In recent years I have frequently been asked by the booksellers of Hilton Head Island to do a coffee-table book about the Island. Whenever anyone uses the expression, "coffee-table book," my immediate impression is of a large, heavy tome equipped with invisible catches which spring out legs, making a table. It's just one of those image things I have. Obviously not what the booksellers had in mind.

*The Sands of Time – A History of Hilton Head Island* was written by me in response to a request by Island book people and has been a popular history ever since its publication in 1989. Given these associations the coffee-table book seemed like a winning pleasure.

Having lived on Hilton Head since 1960, I had many anecdotes to tell. Too often, more than twice-told tales lose more than just their accuracy. Some of the stories were told to me by native Islanders, others by "old-timers" like myself, and a few actually happened to me and my friends. This is a way of passing them along, sprinkled amid outstanding photographs by znaturalist, ornithologist, environmentalist Barry Lowes, some sketches by my husband Walter Greer, and assorted memorabilia shared by many.

The early days of modern development are impossible to relive; so I hope you enjoy the fun of reading about it as much as I did writing it down.

MARGARET GREER
*(August 2004)*

*The mere knowledge that one is on an island, a little world surrounded by the sea, fills one with indescribable intoxication.*

- Lawrence Durrell

*... for where I have gone there are the richest lands for cultivation and cattle-raising... I planted with my own hands grape-vines, pomegranate trees, orange and fig trees...give me some grant of land there, where I might live for always, for it is the healthiest country.*

- Bartolome Martinez, 1577

*... the English that were cast away on that coast in July last were there most part of that time of year that is sickly in Virginia; and notwithstanding hard usage, and lying on the ground naked, yet had their perfect healths all the time. The natives are very healthful; we saw many very aged amongst them. The ayr is clear and sweet, the countrey very pleasant and delightful. And we could wish that all they that want a happy settlement, of our English nation, were well transported thither....*

- William Hilton, 1663

*It is always Sunday on sea islands.*

- DuBose Heyward

*I, a latecomer, hear the waves break still,*
*High tide, by the sea oats, on this quiet shore,*
*And hold an arrowhead picked off the land.*

- Edith Bannister Dowling, 1959

*Left:*
*Oyster Catchers on shell rake*

*Below:*
*Little Blue Heron*

*Nets drying on Skull Creek*

When the word "island" comes to mind,
myriad images swim in the brain:

Beaches

Palm Trees

Lamour

Surf

Sand

Hibiscus

Bali Hai

Sarong

Sunshine

Full Moon

Lagoon

We know an island is what no man is. We also know it is what most men hunger for.

Hilton Head is an island and although it makes a lengthy address, no one living here will sacrifice the identity of the word – or its lure.

Hilton Head Island has 12 miles of beach and an equal amount of gentle surf. Few shells punctuate the smooth beaches, for they have been caught on the numerous sandbars a few miles out, the same sandbars that can snare the unwary sailor. At the same time, heavy waves are diminished as they break upon these 'bars, resulting in an ocean where wind-surfing and sailing in small craft abound. These beaches are lined with palmetto palms and wind-sculptured scrub oaks, but predominantly with tall sea pines.

Smaller, inland pines are not so tall. During the 18th and 19th centuries, the fields where they grow now were cleared for agriculture and in the 20th century used by itinerant farmers to grow large crops of tomatoes. After a couple of "pickings" and shipping, the farmers and laborers moved on, leaving joyous Islanders with all the "vine ripes" they could pick.

At least one or two spreading live oaks were left in every large field, providing welcome shade when resting time came for the slaves or a baby's cries called a mother from the field to suckle her young one. Many of those same oaks which stand today have witnessed Revolutionary War ambush or heard happy singing from Praise Houses as well as a naval bombardment early in the Civil War. These trees shaded the yards of newly-freed slaves who became proud landowners. Other live oaks, clothed in grey veils of Spanish moss, absorb admiring contemplation from millions of Island visitors and shade the roads today same as they did in plantation days.

If you were to ask any native islander what was the single most important day in the history of the island, you might get as many different answers as the number of people you query. Some will say emphatically that it was that day in 1950 when electricity came to the island. "We could listen to a radio!" Other residents will claim the opening of the first bridge in 1956 as the day when easy access made Hilton Head Island a viable place to live for those already here and the tens of thousands yet to come.

A very few might view the Big Picture and advocate the date November 7, 1861. On that day a curtain was lowered on the plantation era, never to return. At the same time the first act of a completely new program began. Within the span of a few short hours, life would change unalterably for those who had a part in it as well as for those who would follow. The plantation owners had filled their slaves' minds about the horrors "Yankee Devils" would do to them. The abandoned slaves hid in the woods and with great temerity slowly came out to greet the Union forces and accept their freedom.

Before 1861 Hilton Head Island had been a site where thousands of slaves worked to raise cotton, indigo, and rice on most of the 25,000-acre island. At least one prominent rice-growing planta-

tion owner had records proving that it took between four to six hundred slaves to work a large rice plantation. With that figure in mind, there must have been at least two thousand slaves on Hilton Head Island at the time of the capitulation of Fort Walker, the site of the battle for Hilton Head in the early months of the Civil War. Plantation owners rarely saw the island, using it mainly as a cool respite from the heat and disease of the towns of Savannah, Beaufort, and Charleston. A superintendent usually ran the very profitable farming on the rich, high land and supervised irrigation of rice fields. The few remaining photographs of native houses prior to the 20th century show dwellings simple but excellent in scale, a tribute in miniature to the superb architecture of the plantation owners' houses in town.

*Facing page:*
*Homestead on Hwy. 278. The house, which stood approximately across from South Island Square, burned in 1965.*

*Above:*
*House on Wild Horse Road.*

*Below:*
*House on Spanish Wells Road. Both houses no longer stand.*

No churches existed for slaves, who were allowed instead "Praise Houses," small, one-room gathering places on each plantation where a few at a time could convene to pray and sing. It was considered unwise to allow them to meet in large groups for fear that insurrection would be plotted. Slave cemeteries are scattered all over the Island, usually somewhere on a plantation site. Of course there were no schools. Keeping slaves uneducated would perhaps keep them quiet, content, and malleable. Such was the thinking of slavery time, used wherever power and control are essential.

By contrast, plantation owners built themselves a wooden church called the Zion Chapel of Ease, located at the crossroads of the Island (Mathews Drive and William Hilton Parkway). It has long ago disappeared, the wooden planks "walking away" to become either fuel or shelter for freedmen after they purchased land, the same land that some of them had slaved on before the Civil War. The Zion chapel in St. Luke's Parish was built shortly after 1786 and the story of its two silver chalices is intriguing.

Made in 1834 by Barnard silversmiths in Paternoster Row, London, the chalices were used in services and give an indication of the great wealth enjoyed by the planters during the Golden Age of the South. During the occupation of Hilton Head by Union forces, both the chalices disappeared. In 1920, the family of a young bride in Philadelphia was searching for old silver goblets to adorn the bride's first home. Finding two old goblets, heavily tarnished, the parents brought them home from the antique dealer, polished them, and were astonished to read from the engraving that they were chalices belonging to a church on Hilton Head Island. At the time, the closest Episcopal Church of full orders was in Beaufort; so the considerate Philadelphia family returned the chalices there with the stipulation that, if ever again there was an Episcopal Church on Hilton Head Island, the chalices would be given to it. They are now used regularly at communion in St. Luke's Episcopal Church on Pope Avenue.

Left:
Zion Chapel of Ease cemetery on corner of Mathews Drive and Hwy. 278, showing Baynard mausoleum.

Below:
In Zion cemetery "is a line of little tombstones, seven simple slabs that give the appearance ... of little ducklings following their mother."

At the burial place at Zion Chapel of Ease, beneath majestic live oaks, gravestones and one mausoleum pay silent tribute to families who braved the rigors of pioneering on an island. There is much to be deduced from reading tombstones if we allow our minds to go back in time and read beyond the chiseled words. One tombstone was written about by David Lauderdale in his *Island Packet* weekly column *That's That*.

"Mary Kirk's epitaph notes that she died a crisp 12 months after her husband 'with whom she had lived in uninterrupted happiness for 43 years.' Uninterrupted happiness? Next to the statuesque tombstone of Mary and James Kirk is a line of little tombstones, seven simple slabs that give the appearance ... of little ducklings following their mother ... It says James Kirk was 'emphatically honest' and that Mary, 'the mistress of a large household, and the mother of many children, guided by the precepts of the Bible, discharged the various duties connected with her position with eminent discretion and success.' ...We also know that Mary was married at 14. At that altar, he (James) would be, at 27, almost twice her age." However, she did live from 1793 to 1851. The Revolutionary War had ended and it had been rather active on Hilton Head with plantation owners who were Patriots fighting skirmishes with the Daufuskie Islanders who were Tories. At the time of Mary Kirk's death, rumors of secession had not begun and the Island was enjoying the most prosperous years ever before. You decide if Mary had "uninterrupted happiness."

No doubt the Kirks met the Baynards on the half-dozen Sundays a year when services were held at Zion Chapel of Ease. Although the Kirks were a few years older, with the few white people living on the Island at the time, they communed at every opportunity. The Kirks would have heard about William Eddings Baynard winning the old Jack Stoney place (Braddock's Point Plantation) in a card game over in Bluffton – or at least that was the way the rumor persisted. Captain Jack Stoney, during the Revolutionary War, was licensed by the new United States to pirate British ships bound from Savannah to Charleston. He did a good job and with the profits built in 1793 the tabby mansion we now know as the Stoney-Baynard Ruins. It makes a good tall tale that the mansion and its surrounding plantation was the prize whose deed Baynard pocketed after the chips were counted in a high-stakes poker game in Bluffton. The loser was the rakish grandson, Captain James Stoney, in 1836. The builder/grandfather (Captain Jack) had died in 1821 and left the mansion to his grandson. The similarity of the two names, Jack and James, has caused many an erroneous historical story to be written. In truth, a Charleston bank held a mortgage on the Stoney-Baynard property.

Baynard's residency was short-lived. He died less than ten years later when he was 49 years old. His wife followed him in death only five years later to be laid to rest along with her husband in the Baynard Mausoleum in Zion Cemetery. A ghostly tale concerning William Baynard's funeral depicts full-moon nights when a funeral cortege proceeds up Plantation Drive in the direction of William

*Tabby ruins on corner of Squire Pope and Gumtree Roads. A few people believe some of the oyster shells may have come from an Indian shell ring across the road. The building itself was not a residence but a storage building for the plantation itself.*

*The Stoney-Baynard ruins in Sea Pines Plantation. Following archaeological digs new and informative signage was put in place in 2004.*

Hilton Parkway. The rattle of the wheels of the black funeral carriage and muted sounds of voices can be heard. At intervals along the way, the carriage stops and William Baynard, silvery and ghostly, leaves the carriage and pauses on the roadside. Plantation Drive today follows almost exactly the course of the original plantation road.

Whatever the tales and suppositions, it is people like the Kirks and the Baynards, all the way to the pioneering of Charles Fraser in his development of Sea Pines Plantation, who have made a difference on Hilton Head Island. Unquestionably, the answer to the financial phenomenon that has been and is Hilton Head Island lies within the men and women who have elected to live and work here. Certainly the native islander plays a large part in keeping the land and providing unusual continuity of human habitation.

# Rattle Weeds

Dolphin Head on Port Royal Sound in Hilton Head Plantation is one of the most beautiful places on the Island. The point of land with its high bluffs has attracted adventurers from the time of William Hilton to the present-day picnic-and-walk bunch.

Getting there, if you are so fortunate as to have a pass or be a resident of the Plantation, is easy today. But it wasn't always so. Before the Plantation was developed in 1972, getting there was a "maybe."

The best way was to start at the end of Squire Pope Road and follow a narrow, sandy road past a spreading live oak and far-reaching tomato fields, fields that had grown long-staple cotton, and would become golf fairways. Although we knew the way was long, the true meaning of "a country mile" or two best explains the distance. Coffee weeds and rattle weeds grew above the roof of the car. Few people had four-wheel drives back then. All we knew was to travel about two miles to the largest clump of rattle weeds (how to measure that?) and turn left. If we turned left too soon, and this we did on several occasions, we ended in a serendipitous situation at the old dock of Seabrook Plantation. Not a bad stop, for in the banks along Skull Creek were layers of oyster shell scattered with pieces of blue-and-white everyday dishes used a century before by the Seabrook family and plantation workers. You could also see why, along these high banks, old maps show a "Careening Point" where pirates and others to follow would careen their ships and boats for cleaning.

But our destination is Dolphin Head; so it is back to the sandy, rutted road and a search for the right cluster of rattle weeds. More often than not, the low-slung cars of the time became stuck in sand or mud before finding the right, or rather left, turn. Here is where another wild bush or small tree came in handy. Using a machete, we chopped away a few fragrant myrtle branches; stuffed the branches

Looking north at Dolphin Head.

Dolphin Head, 1963

under the rear wheels of the car; gunned the engine; and prayed. No other vehicle would come along to help, of that we were certain.

Bumping back on the right trail to Dolphin Head, we knew we were near as openings appeared in the tall grasses and bushes. The real Dolphin Head entrance was at an enormous Toothache Tree. Down through the ages this tree's knobby bark has been used to anesthetize the jaw of someone suffering from toothache. Not as good as novocaine but better than nothing.

Standing on the high bluffs you can see the sweeping view across Port Royal Sound to Parris Island to the left and Bay Point to the right. These are the bluffs sighted by Captain William Hilton from his ship, the Adventure, when he named Hilton's Head. These are the bluffs where Indians camped. This is the site where the Elliott family built their Island home on their Myrtle Bank Plantation. Their main house was in Beaufort. The sound of history demands that you tune in and explore.

Erosion has taken a heavy toll on the bluffs. Prior to the development of Hilton Head Plantation and the addition of a bulkhead at Dolphin Head, the bluff was washing away at the rate of a foot a year. In the 1960s the tabby ruins of Elliott's plantation could be seen at low tide not far out in Port Royal Sound. Today they have vanished. With the erosion, however, square pieces of "furniture" were carved out of the clay banks. Perfect for picnicking.

For those who wanted a picnic on the long, narrow beach that reaches back to the entrance to Skull Creek, a short walk was necessary. Always there was a special reward for the alert. My greatest reward was an Indian spear point, almost camouflaged by shells. Months later, when I showed a friend the place where I found my treasure, there was another one for her. That particular hunter must have dropped his whole bag that day.

A long walk on the beach, a climb over downed live oaks, a delicious lunch, and the time always came to return home. Now if we could just find the right sandy pathway.

Indian spear point camouflaged among seashells.

# "When Gun Shoot"

On that day in 1861, a day that native islanders call "When Gun Shoot" or just "Gun Shoot," the largest armada yet mounted in the United States gathered outside the shoals at the entrance to Port Royal Sound. A Civil War had begun the previous April when Confederates fired on Fort Sumter in Charleston harbor. Although retaliation against South Carolina, the first state to secede from the Union was part of it, the true reason for sending such an overpowering force to take Hilton Head Island was to blockade the entire southeast Carolina coast, rendering shipping from Savannah and Beaufort impossible.

A few miles up the Coosawhatchie (pronounced Coo-saw-hatch-ie) River which empties into Port Royal Sound lay the Charleston-Savannah railroad tracks, defended by General Robert E. Lee. If those tracks were cut, the War could be shortened perhaps by years. But it was to be almost four more years of bloody conflict before Union forces took over this strategic railroad.

General Lee's headquarters were in the Mackey plantation house on the Coosawhatchie River. On Christmas Day, 1861, he penned two letters, one to his wife and one to his daughter. Before he sealed the envelope to his daughter, he picked from the fields outside his tent a small nosegay of violets, pressed them inside the fold of his letter and sent them on their way. On a visit to the site in 2002, violets still bloomed in the surrounding meadows of a much more modern dwelling.

The letter to his wife is as follows:

*I cannot let this day of grateful rejoicing pass, dear Mary, without some communication with you. I am grateful for the many among the past that I have passed with you, and the remembrance of them fills me with pleasure. For those on which we have been separated we must not repine. If it will make us more resigned and better prepared for what is in store for us, we should rejoice.*

*As to our old home, if not destroyed, it will be difficult ever to be recognized.* (He refers here to Arlington, the site of the National Cemetery in Washington, D.C.) *Even if the enemy had wished to preserve it, it would almost have been impossible. It is better to make up our minds to a general loss. They cannot take away the remembrance of the spot, and the memories of those that to us rendered it sacred. That will remain with us as long as life will last …*

*You must not build your hopes on peace on account of the United States going into a war with England. We must make up our minds to fight our battles and win our independence alone. No one will help us. We require no extraneous aid, if true to ourselves. But we must be patient. It is not a light achievement and cannot be accomplished at once.*

*The enemy is still quiet and increasing in strength. We grow in size slowly but are working hard.*

*Affectionately and truly, R. E. Lee*

To his daughter he wrote:

*Having distributed such poor Christmas gifts as I had to those around me, I have been looking for something for you. Trifles are hard to get these war times, and you must not therefore expect more. I have sent you what I thought most useful in your separation from me and hope it will be of some service. Yet how little it will purchase! To compensate for such 'trash,' I send you some sweet violets that I gathered for you this morning while covered with dense white frost, whose crystals glittered in the bright sun like diamonds, and formed a brooch of rare beauty and sweetness which could not be fabricated by the expenditure of a world of money.*

*May God guard and preserve you for me, my dear daughter! Among the calamities of war, the hardest to bear, perhaps, is the separation of families and friends. Yet all must be endured to accomplish our independence and maintain our self-government. Your old home, if not destroyed by our enemies, has been so desecrated that I cannot bear to think of it.*

*I pray for a better spirit and that the hearts of our enemies may be changed. In your homeless condition I hope you make yourself contented and useful. Occupy yourself in aiding those more helpless than yourself. Think always of your father. R.E. Lee*

Cattails

Wild Azalea

Wild flowers with poppies in Sea Pines Forest Preserve

Magnolia blossom

Trumpet Vine

Shortly after the firing on Fort Sumter, Confederates had been sent to Hilton Head to build Fort Walker with bulwarks of palmetto logs, proven in the Revolutionary War to absorb cannon balls. In an elliptical attack on that fateful November day, the Union armada circled Port Royal Sound, firing first on Fort Beauregard near Beaufort and then on Fort Walker on Hilton Head as they passed. During four hours of battle, the flagship *Wabash* alone launched 888 beautifully accurate shells. By noon the defending Confederates on Hilton Head knew the battle was lost and fled to the rear where boats awaited on Skull Creek to ferry them to the mainland. They abandoned their flags, still flying, and tents standing. Also left behind were slaves who hid in the woods when their masters abandoned them. They had been filled with tales of horror should they fall into "Yankee-devil" hands, but they came forth with food and information in exchange for hats, abandoned swords, and money. Most of the Union soldiers had never seen a sweet potato, and the slaves, now free, were happy to demonstrate how to cook and serve this vitamin-rich food.

The first order of business for the Union officers was to make sure the Rebels didn't return. Right away Union soldiers became familiar with more of Hilton Head as they built earthworks equipped with cannon on the northwestern side of the Island facing the mainland. They were absolutely certain that the Confederates would counterattack, especially since a few nights after the victory at Fort Walker (now named Fort Welles by Union officers), Confederate soldiers slipped ashore and burned several plantation houses and supplies to keep them from being used by the enemy. No further forays were made except for a raid on Pinckney Island later in the war in which several Union soldiers were captured.

Word spread fast about the Union headquarters on Hilton Head Island. Slaves escaped by bateaux from mainland plantations. Soon the number of "contrabands" of war (as the first emancipated slaves were called) swelled to 3,000.

An Army and Navy town, which they named Port Royal, was born. More troops were sent to the secured area. The imposing Pope house that faced Port Royal Sound became headquarters for a succession of commanding generals. Three hotels, bakeries, drug stores, jewelry stores, bookshops, a photography studio, a dry goods emporium, and two newspapers occupied the sandy streets. The main street, named Sutler's after the people who sold the goods, soon became known as Robber's Row as testimony to the prices charged. The flurry of building continued until Port Royal numbered some 50,000 people. (In the year 2003, the permanent Hilton Head Island population numbered only 37,000.)

A large hospital was erected on the point where Port Royal Sound joins the Atlantic Ocean. Sick or wounded soldiers were brought here by ship. The mortality rate was high. The dead were buried in a cemetery on Union Cemetery Road and remained there until late in the 20$^{th}$ century when they were moved to the National Cemetery in Beaufort, South Carolina.

*Left: A typical old one-room schoolhouse, now restored, at corner of Beach City and Dillon Roads.*

*Below: Man casting net from a boat in quest of shrimp or small fish.*

Above:
Peace beneath an ancient live oak.

Opposite page:
"Swingtime at Little Blue" painting by Walter Greer. The little house, uninhabited, still stands on Wild Horse Road, but the artist has restored it in his "painter's eye."

Little more than a year after the capitulation of Hilton Head Island, news for the former male slaves in the Beaufort-Hilton Head area was both good and bad. The bad news was that they were pressed into military service. The good news was they could buy land now; their children could go to schools. Those on Hilton Head had government housing in a place near Fort Walker (Welles) called Mitchelville after the commanding General Ormsby M. Mitchel. Barracks-like structures with communal kitchens and wash houses were constructed of Island pine boards, sawn at the local sawmill. Mitchelville continued as a town into the 1870s and was gradually transformed into a kin-based community by the 1880s. Although General Mitchel only lived four months on Hilton Head Island – he was struck down by yellow fever – his memory lives on and in 2002 was honored in a ceremony held by the native islander community on the site of Mitchelville (now Beach City) and attended by several of the general's descendants.

At first the former slaves resisted authority, certain that military training was just another form of slavery. However their commanding officer, an abolitionist from Worcester, Massachusetts, named Higginson, won their confidence so completely that the recruiting agents were swamped with applications. Within months a regiment was ready for combat. After fighting successfully in Georgia and Florida the 1st South Carolina Regiment, along with the Massachusetts 54th, stormed the Morris Island (outside Charleston) fortification, an action colorfully depicted in the motion picture, "Glory."

When the U. S. government allowed "contrabands" (a term used by occupying forces to designate former slaves) to buy land, the former slaves were primarily able to afford or even want more than 10 or 20 acres, enough to farm for themselves, build a small house, and survive. They had money as a result of sales to military and other Port Royal personnel. They knew how to build the broad-beamed, flat-bottomed bateaux so popular to the area for oystering and fishing. The boat could reach into shallow waters, hold bushels of oysters, and provide a stable platform from which to cast a homemade net for shrimp and small fish. Few wanted to work in a cotton field, believing that cotton fields and slavery were interlaced.

The well-scaled houses were usually whitewashed. Window frames and doors were painted a medium shade of blue to ward off hags, "haints" or whatever evil spirits suspected by the Gullah people. (The origin of the word "Gullah" will be addressed later.) By scraping down to the original paint in the 1960s, a Savannah artist, Ann Osteen, developed a palette of colors called Historic Savannah. She sold the colors to a leading paint manufacturer. She called one shade of blue Ha'int Blue, pronounced "hant" but spelled as if substituting "i" for the "u" in "haunt."

People who had come from other places to the booming town of Port Royal had larger sums of money and larger ambitions when land sales opened December 1, 1863. One thousand acres of Honey Horn plantation sold for $200. The following February, it was re-sold for $10,000, a harbinger of twentieth century real estate profits. But the 1863 land boom was short-lived. Failure to properly propagate long-staple cotton caused land prices to plummet to $15 an acre. A pre-war plantation owner family, the Elliotts, had developed a method for continually turning out the finest long-staple cotton by holding back from each year's crop some of the finest seeds. Seed selection, plus annual enrichment of the earth alternately with crushed oyster shell and marsh muck, made millionaires of plantation owners.

Correspondent Charles Nordhoff of *Harper's New Monthly Magazine* wrote in 1863, "The soil on which the famous long-staple cotton was grown, instead of the rich black mould which I expected to find it, is a pale yellow sand, which seems to you useless for agricultural purposes till you notice that it glistens with white particles, which are the pulverized shells the lime of which gives the soil its strength and substance."

Newcomers to the trade did not know these secrets. Large-scale cultivation of the land here came to an end.

Rice was another extremely labor-intensive crop, grown in the Low Country and on Hilton Head. Both Carolina White and Carolina Gold were cultivated. The seed for Carolina White supposedly came from China, brought back from one of the plantation owners' travels. Carolina Gold has a more definite and interesting origin. World renowned for its superior quality to all other rice throughout the world, it was grown from seed brought to the province of Carolina about 1685. The rice had been grown in Madagascar and a brigantine sailing from that island put in, distressed, to the port of Charleston. The English Captain Thurber,

while his vessel was being repaired, made the acquaintance of Dr. Henry Woodward, the first English settler in the colony. Captain Thurber gave Woodward almost a bushel of rice; Woodward gave some to his friends and after rigorous and costly trials and errors, a great rice aristocracy was born. (An excellent source for learning more about the interesting culture of rice and for tales of the people who cultivated it: find a copy of Duncan Clinch Heyward's *Seed from Madagascar.*)

Government appointee Edward L. Pierce was sent to the area to communicate the condition of former slaves, organize their labor, and provide for them. He reported, "An abject race, more docile and submissive than those of any other locality." However agriculture and learning did begin with great faith, on the part of "contrabands," in their white teachers. Heretofore, these former slaves had farmed the land but always under the supervision of an overseer or "driver."

Northern missionary societies and educators realized early that "contrabands" had never been allowed to learn to read and write and were quick to provide men and women who were equipped to do the job to come to Beaufort and Hilton Head. In 1867 the American Missionary Association had 16 teachers, male and female, divided among Stoney's Fairfield Plantation, Chaplin's Marshland Plantation, Seabrook Plantation and in Mitchelville. Teachers had to be members in good standing of "protestant" churches. One such volunteer, named Eliza Ann Summers, arrived by boat in February, 1867, and was assigned to teach freedmen and their children at Lawton's Six Oaks Plantation, far down a sandy road from Port Royal to what is now Sea Pines Plantation. She was 23 years old. Her school was one of the smaller dwellings on the grounds of the former plantation house located on the site which is now part of Six Oaks Cemetery. Majestic trees, planted during better days for the southern aristocracy, testify to the old name of Six Oaks.

Eliza's letters to her sister in Woodbury, Connecticut, from Hilton Head Island, were collected by a descendant into a book called *Dear Sister* which is now out of print. Letters were delivered by boat to Boston and New York in less than one week. (In the year 2000 the delivery time was about the same, although by air instead of boat.) A typical day in Eliza's life consisted of teaching young children in the morning, older children and adults in the afternoon. She sometimes wrote letters for them in the evening, and every Sunday she taught Sunday School. Although she had a companion female teacher, all social life took place at The Head, as the town of Port Royal was called, ten miles away. When attending a "social," they usually went by buggy on the hard-packed beach.

The Hilton Head plantation owners' houses that remained in 1867 were described as off the ground on posts for air to circulate and either unpainted or whitewashed. One observer compared them to barns on stilts, "Big Houses." Big Houses which remained were The Point (Elliott), Seabrook, Fairfield (Stoney), Lawton and Baynard. Eliza Summers described the Lawton house as a one-and-a-half-story, two rooms up and four down with a center hall and stairs, and a wide piazza across the front. The plantation contained about 40 to 50 slave cabins. A teacher's diet consisted of corn and sweet potatoes which they raised, oysters prepared in all styles, oranges, figs, pomegranates, blackberries, peanuts and even robins which were a delicacy.

*Underlay:*
*Sketch of Six Oaks plantation house.*

*Opposite page:*
*Native islander cemetery near 18th fairway of Harbour Town Golf Links. Modern tombstones mingle with homemade markers which at times include a favorite plate or cup of the deceased.*

Other than pine siding, more prosperous pre-Civil War plantation owners had built the main house of tabby, a substance and process handed down from Spanish colonial settlers. The exact proportions of lime, sea water and crushed oyster shells have been lost and attempts to build with something similar have resulted in a total loss. The word tabby comes from "tapia" a Spanish word which means "to tamp." Wooden holding forms were built and walls of tabby were formed by pouring the mixture into the forms to a depth of about twelve inches. When that portion was "set," the forms were removed and placed on top of the solid tabby, followed by more molds and more pourings until the desired height of the wall was reached.

In her letters, Eliza Summers wrote of work in the fields, involving young children who played "Mine de crow" from dawn until dark in spring to keep the crows from eating young corn. Schools usually closed in May because children had to work in fields. (This custom continued in the rural South until the advent of World War II.) Food was very hard to come by, and if crops failed as they did in three consecutive years, people dropped in the fields from hunger, some dying.

She wrote to her sister about death among the native islanders. The coffin was a simple wooden box, nailed shut. Neighbors and friends washed and prepared the body for burial. The graveside funeral consisted of a chapter from the Bible, a prayer, and all attendants walking to the cemetery singing. A walking stick was placed on the coffin after lowering it into the grave. Each friend threw a handful of dirt on the coffin and then prossessed home, still singing. A washtub was filled with water back at the house; everybody washed hands and went about their chores. Many years later an undertaker occupied a mortuary on Jonesville Road.

Lawton Plantation land had been confiscated in March, 1863, along with twenty other plantations. In October, 1874, Joseph and Martha Lawton redeemed their plantation for $600.

Ownership of land seemed to have been the factor that separated the Hilton Head native from his kinsmen on the mainland rural areas. Today the Hilton Head native islander proudly points to his property as having belonged in his family since freedom came. The smaller perfectly-scaled frame houses began to disappear in the 1980s as more prosperous employment came and were replaced by brick and stucco dwellings, all with beautiful views of navigable water or marshland.

*The story of John Holmes illustrates the life of an average native islander during the hundred years between 1863 and 1963. John Holmes was the grandson of a slave and was born in 1885 in a slave cabin at Baynard Plantation, about where the practice greens of Harbour Town Golf Links are located. He and his family didn't leave that area until after the great storm of 1940 when they moved to higher ground on the west side of Broad Creek. Luxury apartments now cover the land where John and Maggie Holmes led a simple life of subsistence farming and fishing until his death in 1972. He was proud that he and his wife had produced 21 children. "We saved three head," he said with a broad smile, holding up as many fingers while his portrait was being painted by Hilton Head's first resident artist, Walter Greer. The portrait is the property of the Hilton Head Museum and hangs there in a prominent place.*

# A Portrait Speaks

By Jim Orr

The sharp morning shadows of February were stretched across the porch as John Holmes left his house. Inside, his wife Maggie made a few adjustments on the small wood stove and began cleaning up the breakfast table.

The room in which the couple had eaten was very small with a low ceiling. The blue window sills glowed with morning light, and on one wall hung a picture of the Virgin Mary and her baby. Today was the day that the cane grinder would come to grind up the long purple stalks of their sugar cane crop. John Holmes walked down to the bank of Broad Creek where his small bateau was tied to a tree. He tossed a flaming stick into a five-gallon drum full of pine knots and soon he had a small sputtering fire going. He untied the boat, placed the bucket of fire into it, and pushed it into the water.

The wind was cold that morning and blew up the creek with the incoming tide. The old man would have to row across the choppy waters and then follow the boundaries of the marsh about a half mile against the wind and tide.

Across the water at Palmetto Bay a young artist waited on the lee side of the Marina store, sketching the remains of an old bateau in the sunlight, looking for signs of the fisherman. Mr. Holmes had agreed to work for the young man and was to row his boat to the meeting place.

The nature of the work had not been discussed the day before, but Holmes had readily accepted the job. Many types of work sustained the old man's family, from odd jobs to fishing to working the small acreage of crops. What Holmes did not know was that he was about to become a model for a portrait. He had assumed that the work involved fishing because the young artist had told him to wear his fishing clothes.

As the artist scanned the creek, he noticed a few wisps of white smoke rising above the marsh at the water's edge. The smoke trail moved slowly towards the docks but was not accompanied by the sound of a motor. Soon, rowing against wind and tide, John Holmes was at the dock. He did not get out of the boat.

"I've come to tell you that the man is coming to grind my cane, and I can't come to work today." He said it as if there was nothing unusual about the statement.

A question ran through the young man's mind. What land was this, where a man in his seventies would brave the cold wind and rough water to row a mile against the tide. His eyes had been transfixed by the portable heater which exhaled the white smoke.

"I'll pick you up in my car tomorrow, Mr. Holmes," he said. Arrangements were made for the next day's rendezvous.

The young man had plenty to think about that evening. A newcomer to the Island, he had been inspired to initiate his painting career there with a character study of a native fisherman. The previous day he had seen Holmes casting his net in a small creek and had decided that the old man would be a perfect model. He recalled their first meeting.

"Catching any shrimp?" he had asked.

"Mullet. Baby mullet. I got three bags full now."

"Use them for bait?"

"No, sir. A man what comes over from Savannah buys them from me. A nickel a piece, twenty-five cents a hand."

Introducing himself, the artist had said, "My name is Walter Greer. I'm a painter, and I wonder if you could help me with some work tomorrow."

"Oh, yessir, I can work." He pulled some

Spanish moss from an overhanging branch, wiped his hands clean, and shook hands with Greer. "My name is John Holmes."

What had impressed Greer the most was the man's very comfortable manner. An unspeakable (but possibly paintable) message was imparted by the man's smooth face and rough, big hands. The face spoke of serenity and pride, answerable to no man but himself. The hands told of the varied physical tasks that made up the fisherman's daily life. It would be quite a challenge to try to capture even a moment in a progression of such momentum and depth.

In his studio the following day, Greer talked comfortably with his model. He explained that he was going to try to "make a picture" of him and that the only work required of him was to sit still for a while. The only thing that puzzled Holmes was that he was not being painted in his Sunday clothes.

The posturing of the hands was difficult, as Greer wanted to display them in a working gesture. Hands moved to the knees, crossed on the lap, fell to the sides. Nothing seemed natural. Starting over, he had Holmes pick up the end of the cast net and simply drop his hands in his lap. Perfect.

For two days Greer worked, entranced with his subject. Holmes was there twice and continually intrigued the artist with many tales of life on Hilton Head. Strangers were new to Holmes, and although a bridge to the mainland had just been built, they were a rare sight. Each man enjoyed the other's receptiveness, and as Greer sat alone, finishing the portrait, he mused back over the stories he had heard.

Holmes had been born in 1885 and was raised in a community that occupied the southern end of the island. That territory had included, until the Civil War, the Baynard and Lawton plantations, producers of indigo, rice, and sea island cotton.

Now the land was owned by a young corporation called Sea Pines Plantation Company, which was in the process of building the first Island golf course.

After the Civil War, a community of ex-slaves had sprung up along the plantation roads. It was here that John Holmes was born.

At the time that he and Greer were working together, Holmes had not seen that part of the island for twenty or thirty years, except from the water. As the artist chauffeured him down the dirt roads, Holmes excitedly pointed out where his various friends had lived. He took Greer to a weed-covered meadow near the ruins of the Baynard home and kicked around the dirt, uncovering some oyster shells.

"This is where my house used to be," he said.

Greer asked him, "Do you know anything about the big house that used to stand over there?" He was referring to the Baynard home.

"Yes, sir. We always called it the old tabby." He offered nothing more about it.

He recalled that when he was very young there had been a hurricane that had almost buried the south end of the Island in water. The storm had filled the low places with salt water and had closed them off from the sea, affording the people a network of ponds in which to catch salt-water fish. Holmes remembered fishing the ponds for several years.

Later the community had moved to the area known as Spanish Wells in order to be on higher ground and closer to the mainland.

This island was unique, and the closer one came to an understanding of it, the more unusual it became. The message from the fisherman grew stronger as the paint grew thicker. Seven decades of living at the edge of the world were speaking vividly through him, and Greer ached to share this past. He wondered if this first painting of his new home would speak to any more of the strangers crossing the bridge.

A week later, the canvas was dry enough to be moved, and Greer's first showing would be to John Holmes. He arrived at the small house with the blue window frames, and white smoke from the chimney told him that someone was home.

John appeared on the porch with his wife, Maggie, clinging closely behind him. He introduced her to Greer, explaining that he was the picture maker. A comfortable curiosity attended them both as Greer turned his painting to face them. To Greer, this audience was his most important.

John Holmes grinned. Maggie giggled and said only a few delightful words.

"He looks just like he's about to speak!"

*John Holmes, subject of the portrait "Noon on Broad Creek," tells artist Walter Greer about Holmes' life before the bridge from the mainland. The conversation occurred at Holmes' house about 1961. (photograph by Bob Smeltzer)*

Several elderly islanders described the hurricane of 1940. "The morning sky was purple with much rain and wind; the tide was so high it drowned livestock in the yards. It took the ferry boat all the way to Bull's Island." Trees 18 to 20 inches in circumference were carried from the Atlantic Ocean to what is now the William Hilton Parkway.

As severe as was the storm of 1940, another hurricane struck the area and did far more damage in 1893. An estimated 1,000 people were killed on the islands between Savannah and the Edisto Inlet. "It is an ill wind turns none to good" as the 16th century saying states. In this case it brought Joel Chandler Harris, the author of Uncle Remus stories, back to the South. He was sent to the Port Royal area which included Beaufort, St. Helena and Hilton Head Island by *Scribner's Magazine* to write about the devastation. Perhaps, as a result, his memories of the Gullah dialect spoken by lowcountry island natives were refreshed, and we have the tales of Buh Rabbit to add to our libraries.

The Library of Congress taped in 1949 the Animal Tales Told in the Gullah Dialect and prefaced the accompanying "translation" with a few words about the narrator, Albert H. Stoddard, and the Gullah dialect itself. Mr. Stoddard was born and raised at his parents' Melrose Plantation on Daufuskie Island where his constant companions were the Gullah people. When a representative of The Library of Congress was seeking someone to record these stories in the dialect, they naturally searched for a native islander who spoke Gullah. Upon hearing Albert Stoddard speaking to some of his friends, they realized that he had the dialect to perfection and he was persuaded to do the job.

*"Conversation in a Winter Garden," a painting by Walter Greer. Work always goes more pleasantly with a companion. Two women till the earth in preparation for a spring garden.*

*Opposite page: Hand-picked "single" oysters are very special. Before and during the early days of modern development, oysters on the island were easy to harvest. Here an oyster man is at work on the site where Harbour Town apartments now stand. (photograph by Bob Smeltzer)*

Gullah has its roots in African and English words. It is believed by some that slaves who were brought from the west coast of Africa and deposited in the West Indies picked up the English of their masters and mixed it with the slaves' native Angolan, the language of the majority. A corruption of the word Angola became Gullah. Cornelia Bailey and Christina Bledsoe, in their book "God, Dr. Buzzard, and the Bolito Man," state: "As to the labels 'Geechee' and 'Gullah,' there's a line of thinking that they came from two neighboring tribes in West Africa – the Kissi, pronounced 'geezee,' who lived where the modern-day coun-

tries of Sierra Leone, Liberia and Guinea converge; and the Gola, a tribe on the Sierra Leone-Liberia border. A lot of members from both of these tribes were brought to these islands (the Sea Islands), and while it has never been proven…it could very well be that what we were called stemmed from the two tribal names."

Brought to the isolated Sea Islands, slaves could speak their melodic language unassailed from the outside world and create a folk culture unlike any other found in the South. Some names on Hilton Head have been corrupted by Gullah people who could neither read nor write and relied on oral repetition. Honey Horn evolved from the name of the family (Hanahan) who owned the place at one time.

Before the first bridge to the Island was opened in 1956, life was hard but simple with philosophies to match. An old native said, "Never hurry, never worry, and always eat before you get tired." Another said, "You can't do anything about yesterday or tomorrow. You can only live right now." Bartering was the economic system – your chicken for my bushel of corn. Owning your own piece of land, knowing what would grow on that land, having a few pigs, chickens, maybe a cow, certainly a marsh tacky horse and a creek nearby – that was all required for the good life of freedom. For some. Within two generations, the lack of educational and employment opportunities caused many young islanders to leave for education after the 6th grade and find a good job in town. By 1930 the population of native islanders had dwindled from a high of 3,000 down to only 300.

The town of Port Royal had celebrated lavishly when General William T. Sherman took Savannah and sent Abraham Lincoln a telegram giving the president the city as a Christmas present. Sherman's march on Columbia and Charleston began on January 25. His troops destroyed everything in their path. Both cities fell on the same day, February 17, 1865.

When General Robert E. Lee surrendered a few months later in Virginia, the Civil War ended and Union troops were withdrawn from Hilton Head Island with suppliers of every nature following.

Only the occupants of Mitchelville and those who had purchased land remained, about 3,000 people. The buildings, the hospital, the hotels, the post office – all just "walked away" board by board and went into the houses for new landowners, as well as churches, and small schoolhouses. By 1872 the name of the post office was no longer Port Royal but had been changed back to Hilton Head Island.

Aside from the gigantic storm of 1893, life on Hilton Head was quiet, a sort of recovery time, privacy for the freed people and a chance for them to accustom themselves to being totally self-sufficient.

For those islanders who did not have a bateau with a sail or wanted to get to Savannah more quickly, an enterprising man named Charlie Simmons bought a 35' power boat which he called *The Lola* and docked it at Big Hole off Broad Creek. A round trip that had in the past taken two to three days by sail, now could be done in 3 hours or less one way. Simmons made the run three times a week in the 1930s. Islanders took produce to the Savannah market which was located two blocks from the river. Today at the market location, Savannah offers a lively place to shop, stroll, or dine.

# The Devil Gun

Activity at the site of the old Confederate Fort Walker again occurred at the beginning of the 20th century. As part of the shore defenses in the United States, the last one of thirteen enormous cannons was installed. It was tested in 1901. According to a report directed to the Chief of Ordnance, U.S. Army, in Washington, D.C., the gun was fired 53 times under a pre-established procedure and must have been fired a number of times prior to the test and also afterwards, pushing the number of firings up to perhaps 100. Popularly called a steam gun, the fifteen-inch cannon was actually a compressed air machine which propelled a dynamite-loaded projectile out of a long tube. Dynamite had been invented in 1868. Bob Insley, who now conducts a weekly tour of the gun emplacement for the Coastal Museum, compares the principle to the BB gun. The ruins of the concrete emplacement are still visible at Port Royal Plantation beach.

As a human-interest story connected with the gun emplacement, a 1957 interview of an 85-year-old Hilton Head man by a Beaufort reporter representing the Charleston *News and Courier* stated that the man had been hired with a friend to "wheel sand in a barrow from the beach to a concrete mixer." When the experimental "devil gun" was finally fired, he and his friend were the only workmen small enough for the barrel-cleaning chore.

"They pulled us through on ropes," he recalled. "No'm, they didn't wrap us in anything. They just pulled us while us hol' the ropes."

The subject of the interview had to be 29 years old when this unusual job was assigned to him, no doubt a rather small-framed person to fit into a fifteen-inch barrel.

Breakfast for Carolina Wrens

Yellow-crowned Night Heron

A Convention of Snowy Egrets

Great Blue Heron

# The First Lighthouse

Prior to building the Steam Cannon, the United States Government also built a lighthouse at Leamington Plantation. It was activated in 1880 with two lighthouse-keepers' houses situated at its base. According to an application by the Coastal Museum of Hilton Head to the National Register of Historic Places, the station was used "as part of a system of navigation lights guiding shipping in Port Royal Sound." The complex included a small brick oil house and a keeper's house and a forward beacon which was mounted on a second keeper's house. The system was taken out of service in the 1930s and its metal frame and tower began rusting away, unused and unoccupied. Prior to and during World War II, Marines from Parris Island, as early as 1938, were sent here as an advanced training camp for anti-aircraft units and defense battalions. The site was named Fort McDougal. Marines camped around the base of the old Leamington lighthouse, built gun emplacements which occasionally still surface at low tide on the beach at Palmetto Dunes, and rode around the roads of Hilton Head in the backs of trucks, bayonets fixed. The frightened native islanders blamed just about

*A major Hilton Head road around 1940.*

everything bad on them. The Marines' time on Hilton Head did coincide with the vandalism of the Baynard Mausoleum, but so did the time in 1942 when the Coast Guard had a Mounted Beach Patrol Training Center here. According to a participant in the operation, the camp accommodated several hundred men and "100 or more horses and dogs." Sometime during the years of training consisting of many people, a small group broke down the marble doors to the mausoleum, dragged the

*Artist's conception of Leamington Light Station c. 1885.*

iron caskets outside, and dumped the remains into the nearby marsh. The more intrepid ones climbed one at a time inside the caskets, had their friends lower the lids and make their pictures, eyes closed, with their faces showing through the glass in the lids. The iron caskets were then thrown into the marsh, to be rescued a decade later by the Hack family and stored in a barn until a museum was formed on Hilton Head in 1985.

Leamington Plantation, which had belonged to a member of the Pope family originally, was later purchased by 44 members of the North Carolina Hunting Club. They sold it in 1966 to Greenwood Development Company which re-named the property Palmetto Dunes. Later the company parceled off a section for the exclusive area now known, once again, as Leamington. Greenwood Development has carefully restored the Leamington Light in a park-like setting.

*Opposite page and below:*
*Derelict lighthouse.*

*Below:*
*Restored lighthouse in Leamington Plantation.*

# The Blue Lady

As for the Leamington lighthouse-keepers' houses, their story continues to the present day. When Charles Fraser was building Harbour Town in Sea Pines Plantation in the mid-60s, he bought the two houses and had them moved to the woods surrounding the construction of the harbor where a two-lane sandy road was built through heretofore untrammeled territory. Of course the very isolation of the place attracted the home-from-school white teenagers at holiday time. Two young men and two young women, on Christmas holiday, drove down one night to the area of the lighthouse-keepers' houses. One of the young men raced home, burst into his parents' bedroom near midnight, and exclaimed, "Wake up! You won't believe what I just saw!"

When his mother turned on the bedside light, she saw her son with his hair windblown and his face whiter than she had ever seen. He insisted on telling his mother and father everything that had transpired. Well, almost everything.

"Four of us decided to go down to where Harbour Town is being built," he said. "We saw these two abandoned houses and drove over near them. We were going to go inside them when, all of a sudden, a long tapering blue light appeared in the window. We all saw it. Then the light drifted to another window. It was like a veiled person, a lady. When the light came out on the porch and moved in our direction, we all jumped in the car and drove away as fast as we could. Mom, I think some of the older boys are trying to play a trick on us. In the morning will you go down there with me and let's see if we can find some footprints or something? And since you and Dad are awake, can I make a pallet on the floor and sleep in here?"

The morning sunshine produced no clues as

*Opposite page: Artist Walter Greer's concept of The Blue Lady.*

to the unusual phenomenon. No footprints, no broken branches or trodden bushes, no pulleys. The boy talked of little else for the remainder of his holiday; so when his parents were telling another couple one night about the incident, the four of them decided to see for themselves. Skeptical to say the least, they quietly sat in their parked car near the houses in the deep woods. Almost immediately, a blue apparition emanated from one of the windows and floated to another window as the adults watched. Their vigil was brief. They left more quickly than they had arrived. Later that night at the parents' home, a portrait of a beautiful woman fell to the floor, face down. The Blue Lady appeared to be a jealous woman.

When spring vacation came, the same four young people gathered their courage, added a tape recorder, and waited for midnight to go to the lighthouse-keepers' houses. This time they vowed to go inside at least one of the houses. With only the car lights to help them find the front steps and a flashlight for inside, one of the girls started up the pulled-down attic steps. The recorder was on. On the tape could be later heard, "She's calling me up the steps." "I wouldn't go up there if I were you." "But she insists. She's pulling me." The girl kept going up, slowly, breathing heavily, while her companions kept insisting she come down. Suddenly, there was a piercing scream from the girl and she fell backwards down the stairs to be caught by her friends. "She pushed me!" she hysterically yelled.

The boy played the tape for his parents who were more than a little inclined to believe. He also said he had no intention of going back to the houses.

The visits stopped and construction of Harbour Town continued. The tale of The Blue Lady grew. Recollections were resurrected. In various versions, the story of the Leamington Lighthouse keeper, a widower named Adam Fripp, remains basically the same. Fripp had a 20-year-old

*Opposite page:*
*One of the "keepers" houses at the original site.*

*Above:*
*When the two houses were restored and moved to their present location, a small brick courtyard was built between the houses and named The Court of The Blue Lady.*

*Bottom:*
*Open for business. Restored lighthouse keeper's house in Harbour Town*

daughter, Caroline, who was forced to keep the light for several days, alone, after her father had a fatal heart attack during a storm. The trauma of being compelled to stay in a cramped space over 80 feet above the ground with her father's dead body caused her to sicken and die three weeks later. Was Caroline Fripp, unhappy that her young life had been cut short, still searching for fulfillment as she roamed the houses?

When the two houses were restored and moved to their present location on the right side of the entry road to Harbour Town, a small brick courtyard was built between the houses and the courtyard is named The Court of The Blue Lady.

The same young man who had seen The Blue Lady originally went down one bright moonlight night to see the courtyard. The following morning when his mother questioned him about a thin silver wedding band he was wearing, he told this story:

"I was standing in the moonlight and felt a cool 'presence' sweep past me. I looked down on the bricks and there was this wedding ring. I stooped, picked it up and put it on. The 'presence' brushed my cheek and was gone. I know The Blue Lady left the ring for me."

True or not, The Blue Lady has never been seen – or felt – again.

*Right:*
*Honey Horn Plantation is owned by the Town of Hilton Head Island and has been leased by the Museum The Big House (p. 57) will house historical exhibits.*

Leamington Plantation was not the only place bought by outsiders for the sole purpose of hunting. About 1887 W.P. Clyde, who had been stationed on Hilton Head Island as an enlisted man with the Union Army, set up the Southeast's first privately owned hunting preserve. He was the largest landholder by far at that time on Hilton Head. The Honey Horn Plantation house and its dependencies were the headquarters for the necessary horses and guides. Guests could stay in the Big House. This operation provided employment for native islanders and, for the first time, money became the exchange instead of the barter system. After Clyde's death the land was sold to Ohio industrialist Roy Rainey who, in 1910, sold to New York state residents Landon Thorne and Alfred Loomis. On a much smaller scale hunting continued after the Fred Hack family moved to Honey Horn in 1950 and leased out the rights for hunting. After the first bridge was opened in 1956, most of the horses were sold and hunting abandoned for timbering and development.

Miss Beatrice Milley became postmistress in 1942 and told about life on Hilton Head before the bridge. Her post office was in a small frame building almost opposite the first consolidated school building. The post office building became many things: a health center, the Sheriff's office, voting headquarters. When it was abandoned, vines took over and the small structure slowly crumbled into the ground.

Mail in Miss Milley's time before the bridge was brought by boat. Mail would be delivered by truck to the nearest point on the mainland to Hilton Head, then rowed across by boat three times a week. The first ferry wasn't authorized until 1953. In an interview taped when she was a very old lady, Miss Milley claimed some islanders only collected their mail three or four times a year. Some required the postmistress to read the mail to them, and occasionally some would borrow money from Miss Milley to pay their taxes. She also sent food to hungry relatives "up north."

*Bottlenose Dolphins, happy to be here.*

*Photograph above shows them "strand" feeding, only in the waters around Hilton Head Island.*

# The Last Monkey

Late one April afternoon in 1958, a native island farmer saw something moving around in his corn crib. He grabbed his shotgun, charged across his yard and filled the marauder with buckshot. He had just shot the last monkey that had escaped to Hilton Head from Pinckney Colony outside Bluffton.

The Monkey Farm, as the site was called, had been in operation for more than a decade since the late 1940s and was one of the drop-off points for rhesus monkeys imported from India, acclimated to the United States, then shipped to various polio laboratories across the country. By the time the Hilton Head farmer shot the monkey in his corn crib, Jonas Salk and Albert Bruce Sabin had perfected the preventive for the dreaded poliomyelitis and grateful parents were taking their children to clinics everywhere to receive their cube of sugar with the wonderful medicine drizzled on it, medicine that would allow children to enjoy a summer with their peers, unafraid of the maiming and sometimes fatal disease that had plagued them for so long.

Questions still surround the "escapes" of these monkeys from their cages. A bounty of between $5 and $10 was offered for any returned escapee; so it follows that quite a few mischievous monkeys were found enjoying their freedom in this salubrious climate. As late as 1961, golfers on Hilton Head were claiming they saw a monkey. The sighting usually turned into a grapevine twining around the limb of a tree rather than a tail.

For many years the University of South Carolina in Columbia was custodian of The Last Monkey which they stuffed and named "Mr. Hilton." In 1985 a writer working on a magazine article about the Monkey Farm called the University to see if a photograph could be made of Mr. Hilton to accompany the article. The writer was told that, during a recent move of laboratory equipment to new quarters, formaldehyde was spilled all over the stuffed monkey, altering him beyond recovery.

*THE LAST WHAT?*

Before the bridge to Hilton Head Island was completed in 1956, approximately 800 native islanders lived here, according to oral history tapes. Every community had its own school which educated the children up to the seventh grade. After that they had to leave home and go to Savannah or to Penn School in Beaufort for further education. Nevertheless at least one native testifies that everybody could read and write. It wasn't just go to school and hopefully learn something. In winter the students cut wood for the pot-bellied stove which was the only source of heat in a one-room schoolhouse. They filled a large bucket with water from the pump for drinking from a communal dipper. Two outhouses needed to be cleaned: one for boys, one for girls.

Each community had a store which was certainly the favorite place for children. Visions of candy and soda pop were the light at the end of a long day working at the oyster factory on the sight where the Crazy Crab restaurant is now located. The work ethic was instilled early for all islanders. One lady who was born in 1924 remembers being paid a "nickel for 12 quarts of shucked oysters." Even though her father owned a store and a "pavilion," she asked that her nickel be changed into five pennies. "Make it go farther." She also helped her father in the store when she was so small she had to stand on a crate to reach even the lowest shelves.

*Opposite:*
*Life on Hilton Head before the bridge as depicted by Walter Greer in his painting of Owens Grocery.*

*Above:*
*CHARLEYWIGGINS ROADSIDEMARKET, a Walter Greer painting of the store and house on Hwy. 278.*

# Sarah Grant

By Robert Hanie

*(The story of Sarah Grant, Daufuskie Island midwife, is also a story of other midwives who lived and practiced their skills on Hilton Head as well. The story of Sarah Grant was published in 1974 in a book called "Gaule, the Golden Coast of Georgia." The publishing group, Friends of the Earth, has graciously consented to the re-printing of this story.)*

The road to Sarah Grant's house on Daufuskie has writing on it – worm scribblings, the bounding quotation marks of deer, snake slithers, centipede wanderings. The worms have the most to say. Their task is to loosen the soil, let air and water in, and turn the earth over so that it can spring again. Theirs is a monumental reshaping, and the energy for it is only hinted at in the crazy scribbling. Lois Faye Robinson, eight years old, her hair sprigged with a blue ribbon, leads the way to Sarah's house, her bare feet footnoting the worms' epic message. To her left and right are bipetaled blue dayflowers, like butterflies beside the road, and the smell of horsemint is all around her.

Sarah Grant is an eighty-six-year-old midwife. She lives in a blue-shuttered, earth-colored bungalow with a crippled cat, a dog, and a horse named Tillman. The bungalow is surrounded by small vegetable tracts, some outbuildings, and a leaning barn in which several dusty coffins are stacked. "My husband was the undertaker," Sarah says "I brought them into the world and he took 'em out, as people used to say." Today Sarah spends her time in a faded white rocking chair on her tiny porch, warmed by the sun. Talking to Sarah is like assisting at a difficult delivery. It starts slowly but finally comes. Listening to the sound of her voice, you can hear her talking to all the women she has helped through childbirth – tones of assurance, strength, understanding, and joy.

"One hundred and forty," she says. "I think it's one hundred forty. I lost track. You can check the records at Bluffton – only two died. I started in 1932. The last – the last one was Ella Mae Stevens in January 1969. They go to the hospital in Savannah now and I ain't sorry a bit. They can do better at the hospital.

The Lord and I do it together. People come and get me in a car or wagon. Sometimes I get there too late – the baby's waiting on me. First thing I do is cut the cord and tie it and dress it. Then I put the baby on a pallet. I wash his head and oil him all over – I don't wash the rest of him for two weeks. The baby comes in a 'bed.' There's another bed in the mother. Sometimes it doesn't come and you gotta get that bed out. Once the bed didn't come out for a week and I had to get the doctor – that's the only time the doctor came in thirty-seven years. When that bed comes you tend to the mother, then after that you tend to the baby. Then the mother nurses the baby. Sometimes there's no milk and we have to make a sugar teat. Yes, I think how they take the breast tells you something of the person they will be. But not all the time. Sometimes they are greedy when they start, but not later. Take Joe Bryan. He was a water baby. He was born on the water, in a boat. We were on the way to Savannah. I had everything with me. He came about half way over. We turned around and went right on back. He didn't cry – too scared to cry. Some do come crying. Some come quiet. Some come fighting. Children don't be like they used to be. Used to be they'd keep their eyes shut for a long time. The children who come now look around with their eyes wide open. They got sense. Take the little Sullivan boy – he's the littlest one at the school now. He come like a dead child – limber. I gave him up for dead. But he didn't – a good while later he circulate about. He came foot foremost – when they come foot foremost they say he's going to be a wise fellow.

"I didn't use forceps, just my hands. Nothing else. Doctors use clamps and all kinds of things. Mine come by nature. Let it come by nature. Nature put it there – let nature bring it out. Let it come by nature. Sometimes the women do cry. Sometimes they get scared and cry. No, I don't give them drugs. I give them one pill to help them to go to sleep when it's all over."

Sarah went inside and brought out her tiny black leatherette bag, frayed at the edges. "I got this in Beaufort when I started in 1932," she said, unzipping the bag and taking out her surgical gown, folded neatly after her last birth in 1969. She placed it on top of the kit. "That's my gown, and those are my hand towels. That's my cotton. I got everything I need right here. My lysol, my soap, my handbrush. That's my tray to sterilize my scissors, and this is what I weigh the baby with." She held up a tiny, spring-operated scale. "That's my baby oil, that's my scissors, that's my eyedrops, and that's my eyedropper. This is my tape and paper to dress the baby's cord , and this is my pills. I give them one to take after they eat. We always give

*Above:*
*Trumpet Vine*

*Below left:*
*Cherokee Bean*

*Below right:*
*Daffodils*

them ham and eggs, biscuits and grits and coffee after it was all over."

Folded in half at the very bottom of the black bag was Sarah's "Midwives Certificate of Registration," issued under the laws of the State of South Carolina for the year 1968. She proudly pointed to the back, where the "Rules and Regulations Governing Midwives in the State of South Carolina," were listed.

"I got ten dollars back then, in Beaufort when I started, and I had to split that between two of us. It got to be thirty dollars for me along by the time I quit, but it's worth more than that. It takes a lot of work. Some years you don't have none. Some years several. Some years you have five or six. They're all over, now. Some's in New York, some's in Miami, some's in Detroit."

Sarah enters her house, as neat inside as her midwife's kit. The kitchen, with its woodfired, cast iron, knuckle-footed stove ("Universal Stove, Rome Cooperative Foundry, Rome Georgia") is immaculate. Sarah busies herself there for a moment, then reappears on the porch, pushing the screen door open with her foot and carrying out a silver tray heavy with two cut-glass wine goblets and a bottle each of V.S.O.P. brandy and Samovar Vodka, with paper napkins folded into triangles and stuck between. "My brother gave me those wine glasses in 1913 for my wedding," she says. "He died of influenza at Camp Jackson during the First World War. He gave me six. Three's left." The brandy is eight years old, but only about an inch is gone from the neck of the bottle. The liquid in the vodka bottle is purple.

It's God's medicine," Sarah says. "We make it from the berries here on the island."

# The Good Old Days?

For better or for worse, this simple life was about to end although it was another twenty years in the coming. In 1950 a syndicate of Georgia lumbermen bought nineteen of the twenty-five thousand acres on Hilton Head Island for the purpose of timbering the tall, long-leafed yellow pines. The four principals were Fred Hack, C.C. Stebbins (his father-in-law), Olin McIntosh, and Lt. General Joseph B. Fraser. General Fraser's son Charles was, at the time, a Yale law school student and at any vacation time he was put to work driving a logging tractor on the newly purchased land. Although young Fraser basically covered all the island, he seemed to be more and more on the south end. As he drove along in the heat, slapping mosquitoes, he looked at the pines and the massive oaks, the meandering creeks and swampy areas and the dream that would years later become Sea Pines Plantation was germinated in his head. He thought an upscale development would be a good thing to do – for someone else. But by the time he completed his law training and served two years in the Air Force, he had changed his mind. He bought 4,000 acres on the south end of Hilton Head Island from his father for $600,000 in 1956 and then added 1,200 acres which he bought from other syndicate members for $1 million. The groundwork for an entirely different type of land development, based on environmental considerations and not a Monopoly board, had been laid. Armed with a master land plan, and with the advantage of a bridge that had just been opened to the island, Charles Fraser began the long road of raising vast sums of money for heavy machinery and publicity, all the unimagined accessories to building a community and getting compatible people interested in coming. He built a house for himself on Green

Heron Road and hired a few bachelors, like himself, to work for him. He needed a vice-president, a public relations man, and of course a real estate salesman. The Sea Pines Plantation office was in a trailer at Sea Pines Circle. A mobile telephone occupied a unique telephone booth – an old car rigged so that when a call came in, the car horn honked. Whoever was least busy in the office would go outside and answer the phone. Telephone service was not brought to Hilton Head until 1960 by Mr. and Mrs. Harvey whose descendants still run the company. Two years would pass before the

first deed was signed in 1958 to buy a Sea Pines lot. Nevertheless, within this ambitious land plan, a Forest Preserve of over 600 acres was set aside and gratis land was made available to churches along Pope Avenue.

A 40-room William Hilton Inn was built to provide lodging for those interested in purchasing property and later served as a sort of "clubhouse" for early residents. Those residents were requested to be present at Charles Fraser's house every Saturday evening to "screen" prospective buyers. If those buyers were not considered proper neighbor material, real estate salesmen politely told them the following day that there was nothing on the market at that time and that they would be called when something came up. The six-to-eighter cocktail party was born on Hilton Head.

Now Charles Fraser's father, the General, was a staunch Presbyterian and frowned on the serving of any alcoholic beverages. Matilda was Charles' faithful maid. The bridge was manned by a tender who perched atop the swing bridge in a small cubicle and opened and closed the bridge should any traffic come over with someone willing to pay the $2.50 toll. Should the General arrive, the tender quickly notified Matilda to "lock up the liquor; the General's on the island." If this should occur on a Saturday, the party was moved to a married employee's house a block away.

Another very special form of hospitality was offered at the William Hilton Inn. All the rooms opened to an outside walkway and room service trays were placed outside for pickup. Unerringly stray dogs which inhabited the Island knew exactly when breakfast or lunch was over and would appear on the walkways to clean the plates which guests had placed outside. The Hilton Head Humane Society, along with all other community organizations, was yet to be formed.

Following Fraser's example, Fred Hack developed Port Royal Plantation and Olin McIntosh persuaded a large contingent of Savannah people to join him on Bram's Point and the Spanish Wells area. While not exactly running a race, Hilton Head Island was off the mark and making a name for itself nationally.

The original Sea Crest, an oceanfront motel with ten rooms and no keys, was built by Wilton Graves in time for the bridge opening. Until the mid 1970s islanders did not lock the doors to their houses or remove the keys from their cars. Most of the time a wallet was not needed because there was nothing to buy and no patrolman to ask for a driver's license. Mr. McElveen, whose wife Katie owned the Roadside Restaurant, was the sole law enforcement officer, but he knew everybody and everybody's car. If you bought a new car, you better tell him right away; otherwise you'd be pulled over to the side of the road and questioned.

Stretch your imagination, if you will, and envision a drive from the bridge down Highway 278 to the Sea Pines gate in 1958. (Only an ocean entrance to Sea Pines existed; the Greenwood entrance was a hazardous,

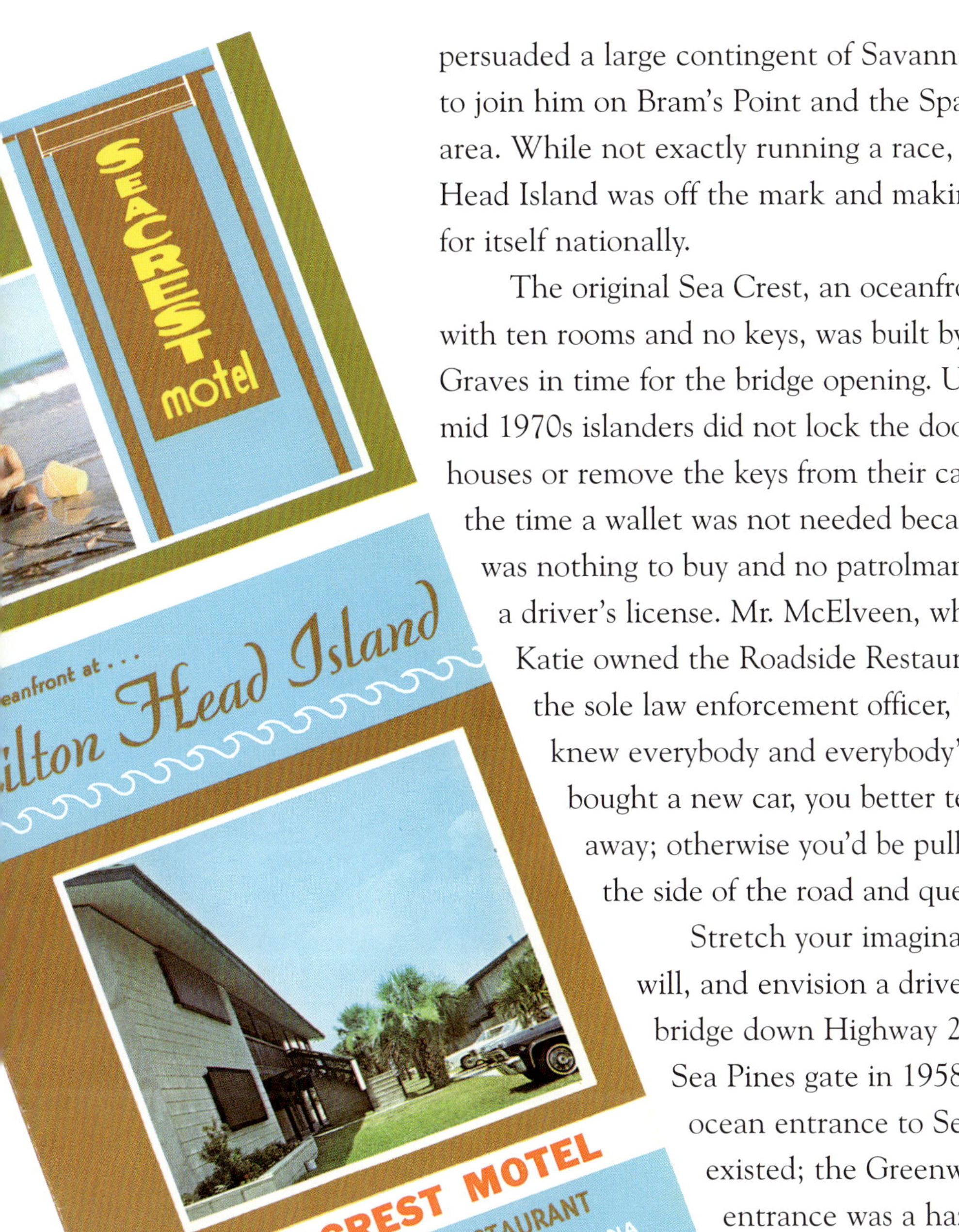


| RATES EFFECTIVE TO March 1, 1969 | March 1 to September 15 Oceanfront | March 1 to September 15 Poolside | September 15 to March 1 Oceanfront | September 15 to March 1 Poolside |
|---|---|---|---|---|
| Room with two double beds | | | | |
| Daily - Double | $ 17.00 | $ 15.00 | $ 14.00 | $ 12.00 |
| Three or Four persons | 20.00 | 17.00 | 17.00 | 15.00 |
| Two bedroom apartment, kitchen, living area. Sleeps six persons. Reserved weekly only, but will rent by the day if vacant on arrival. | | | | |
| Weekly | $165.00 | $145.00 | $135.00 | $120.00 |
| Daily (if available) | 27.50 | 24.50 | 22.50 | 20.00 |
| Kitchenette with one double bed and one single bed. Reserved weekly only. | | | | |
| Weekly | $125.00 | $110.00 | $110.00 | $ 95.00 |
| Daily (if available) | 20.00 | 18.00 | 18.00 | 15.50 |

Try us for that plush vacation you have always wanted, now that you know anyone can afford it at the SeaCREST. Please make reservations early, since the SeaCREST is the only ocean-front Motel with swimming pool on the Island.

We prefer not to have pets.

European Plan Only
Deposit Requested

Check In—4:00 P. M. — Check Out—1:00 P. M.

RATES SUBJECT TO CHANGE WITHOUT NOTICE

*Below left:*
*Faithful customers frequent the fruit and vegetable stand on the site.*

*Bottom right:*
*The Marsh Tacky horse would be either tethered in the field or pulling a plow.*

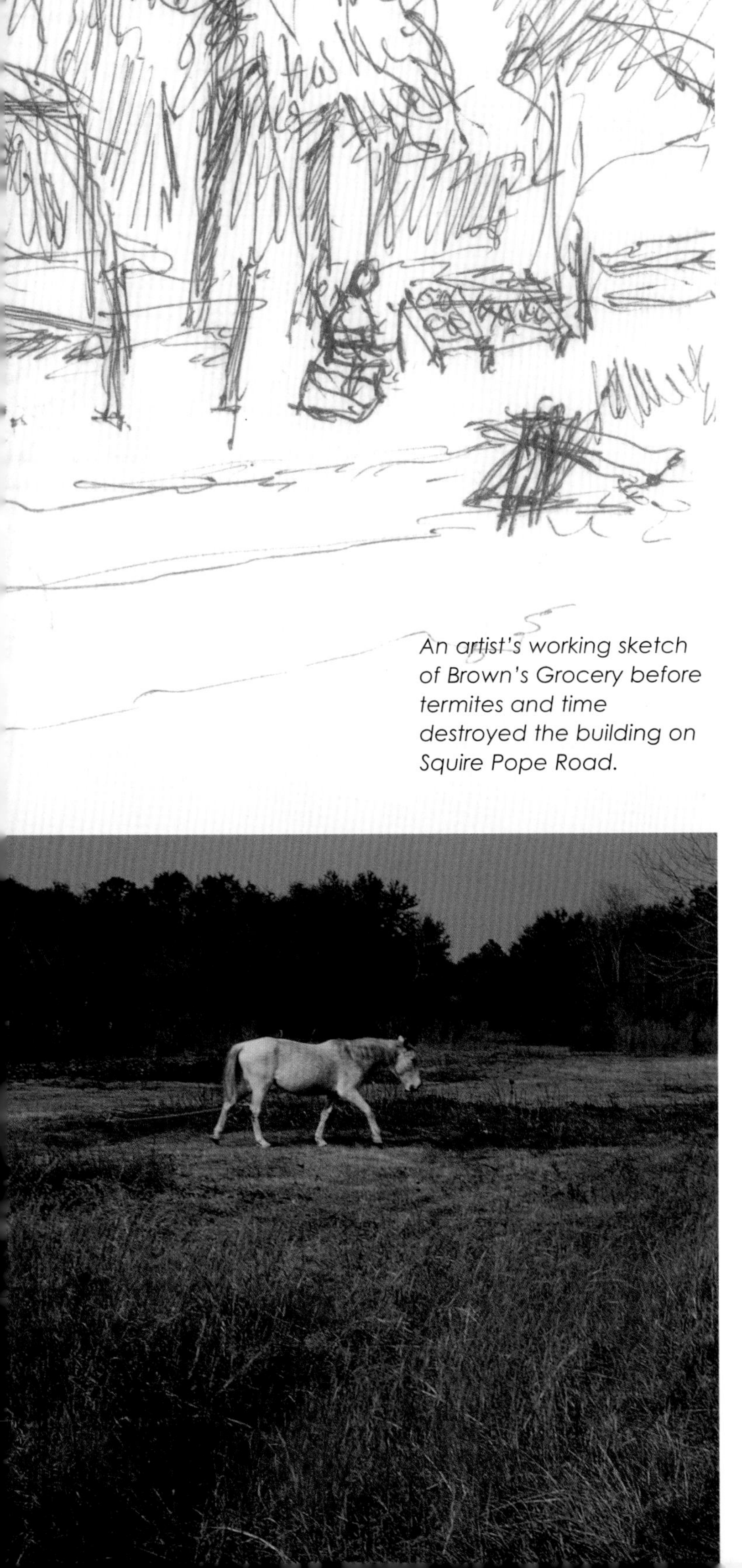

An artist's working sketch of Brown's Grocery before termites and time destroyed the building on Squire Pope Road.

sandy road.) The first thing everyone saw after crossing the bridge was a large billboard advertising Willie Wirehand who brought you electricity courtesy of Palmetto Electric Cooperative. Many years would pass before a county-wide signage law would be passed. Tim Doughtie is the person to thank for getting this law passed. Most days the eleven-mile drive would be pretty lonely with scarcely another car in sight. Just in case, though, islanders kept their right hands at twelve o'clock on the steering wheel and flipped up the fingers in greeting should another vehicle appear. Small houses were on either side of the road, all of them with neatly swept yards with perhaps a collection of chickens pecking away while a dog slept on the front porch. The main activity of the occupants of these houses came from the road; so all porches faced the road with very comfortable chairs thereon. Few cars and trucks were parked in these yards (there were only 11 on the Island in 1950), but nearly all of the yards held a buggy or wagon. Depending upon the time of day or the day of the week, one of the 100 or so Marsh Tackies would be either tethered in the field or pulling a plow. If it were a Sunday mid-day, the horse would be hitched to a wagon in a church yard. In the back of the wagon would be a number of kitchen chairs which had transported the ladies to worship and would supply seating for the picnic to follow on the church grounds. Occasionally one of the horses would be saddled for a quick ride down the road.

Frazier's Temple was on the right side of the road, same as today, and the consolidated brick school building was close by. The Zion Chapel of Ease cemetery is near the crossroads of Mathews Drive and the main road, but, except for the Baynard mausoleum, most of the tombstones were obscured by weeds. On the left side was Folly Field Road which led to 20 cottages built in 1952. On down the road sprinkled with native islander homes was the telephone company office on the

*Overleaf:*
*Queen Anne's Lace is the title artist Walter Greer gave to his painting of the Christopher house that was one of the many native islander houses lining Hwy. 278 in the Fairfield and Chaplin communities.*

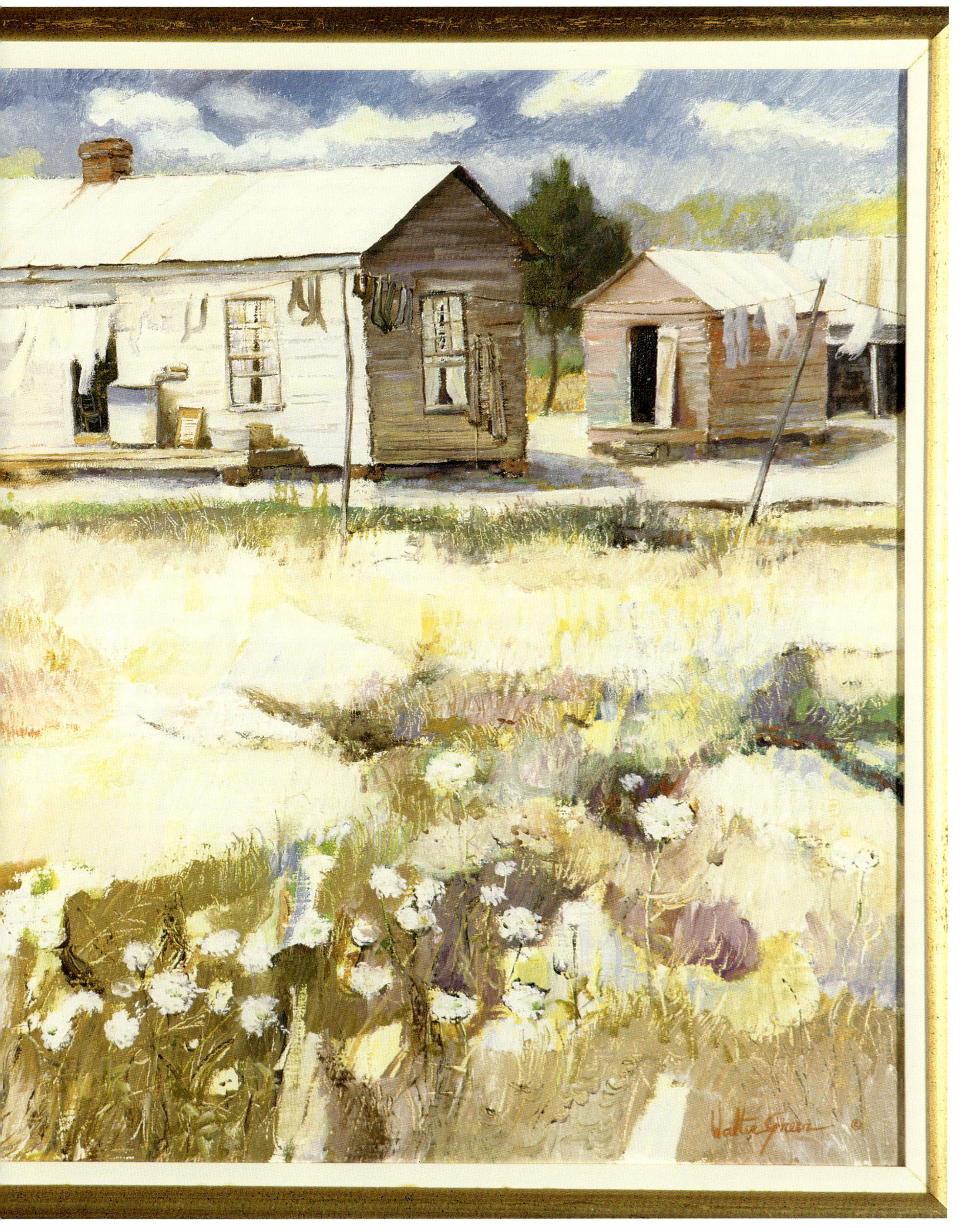
Walter Green ©

right and the Roadside Restaurant across from it. Then nothing until the Sea Pines circle with its offices and then Coligny Circle with its shopping center, filling station, liquor store, grocery store and the Sea Crest Motel. To the right of Coligny Circle and down the beach road was the Arcade, an enterprise with a steam table, cooking facilities and a large refrigerator and a juke box. This building would later boast a miniature golf course and bowling alley and ultimately, around 1966, become the first home of the Montessori School, possibly the only oceanfront pre-school anywhere. Forest Beach vacation homes, simple in construction, could be seen after the nearly completed William Hilton Inn and there you were at the Sea Pines gate, although there was no gate. Just drive on in and you're welcome.

*Above:*
*Postcard of The Arcade, a 1960s enterprise consisting of a small grocery, a juke box, and would ultimately become the first home of the Montessori School before it was torn down to make way for multi-storied, oceanfront apartment buildings.*

The twelfth house was completed in Sea Pines Plantation in 1961, coinciding with telephone service. It was no longer necessary to leave notes on the few doors in case someone was having a party. Everyone was invited to every party because even if they weren't invited, they drove by, saw the cars and came in anyway. Those people who chose to live here without stores and medical

*Opposite:*
*One of the few remaining beachfront houses in the original style.*

facilities thought they were on a permanent vacation in paradise and left only long enough to stock up on food in Savannah, see a movie, get a haircut and hurry home.

Most of the houses hugged the shoreline where the few narrow paved roads were partially silted over with sand. Several people carried three additional items in the trunk of their cars: a tow cable, a machete and a shotgun. The machete was for hacking a path through unexplored territory and the shotgun was to blast one of the many rattlesnakes. (Later they disappeared under the blades of major building machinery.) As for the tow cable, cars were prone to get stuck in the sand on the side of the road and needed a little tug.

Coburg Dairies provided door-to-door deliveries of dairy products and bacon that helped keep the larders stocked between the Savannah food runs. Milk bottles were glass in the early 1960s and housewives left little notes stuck in the tops of clean bottles, deposited on the back steps for twice-weekly pickup and fresh supplies. The notes read something like this: "Please leave 4 quarts of milk, a pound of bacon, one of butter, and put it on our bill."

Bills were rendered monthly. No orders for cream because the milk was not homogenized, bottles were glass, cream rose to the top, and everyone had a cream separator. Everyone also had a freezer – a big one – the kind that little children thought was a great place to keep a body until the undertaker arrived.

# Taking an Alligator for a Walk

By Charles Fraser

We persuaded the *Saturday Evening Post* to send their chief photographer down to Hilton Head Island. They were doing a series entitled "People on the Way Up" – the first woman police chief, or some guy who had climbed up the side of the Empire State Building and slid down – just weird stories! So I was picked as a weird story of someone on the way up.

I remember sitting in the dining room of the Hilton Head Inn with the very distinguished photographer and David Pearson, our public relations director, and I said I wanted my photo taken in front of the inn.

No, he didn't want that.

And I said, "Well, what about down at our golf course?"

Nope, didn't want that.

And I said, "Well, that's what it is we try to get people to know about."

"That's fine," he said, "I'll give you the address of the advertising manager of the *Saturday Evening Post* and you can contact him and you put any picture you want for $50,000 on the page you've bought."

And I said, "We can't do that. We haven't made $50,000 all month."

And he said, "That's your problem, not mine."

And so David Pearson said, "Where do you want Charles for the photo?"

And he said, "I want him dressed as a Yale Law School student, with a Brooks Brothers suit, rep tie, straw hat, rolled umbrella, walking an alligator."

I said I'd never walked an alligator.

David kicked me under the table and said, "Charles would love to walk an alligator. We'll have our gamekeeper catch an alligator for Charles to walk."

Well, you know, our gamekeeper was really the Caterpillar driver. He chased all the small alligators and they all got away. The only alligator that wasn't running was a huge one that we were feeding the scraps from the Hilton Head Inn to every day – all the leftovers went down to this alligator. So he had grown accustomed to people coming around with food.

So they came up with some food, and ropes and lassos, and lassoed this alligator and pulled him up onto the shore. Mad as hell.

And with all sorts of out-of-sight guys with ropes on the gator's tail, out of the camera angle, I was photographed with the part of the alligator that was unchained.

Then we turned the alligator loose and he got up on his legs like a dog and started running down to his pond, goose-stepping. I instinctively started goose-stepping along with the alligator, while the photographer hollered, "Keep it up! Keep it up!"

He was there with his camera, and I was trying to help him get his shot – because if he didn't get it, he was going to go back to Philadelphia.

The shot that actually appeared showed the alligator looking very friendly – open-mouthed and just sort of smiling. One second after that last shot was taken he was lunging at the photographer with his jaws and whipping his tail at me and suddenly both of us were running for dear life. And that was the last time I've gotten near an alligator.

reprinted with permission from *Hilton Head Monthly*

After the William Hilton Inn opened in 1959, it became the clubhouse for residents of the south end of the island. Dinner out was an occasion at least once a week; mail could be picked up at the Inn's desk; or a painting bought from a current art show. In the beginning, dinner was something of an adventure. Not all the kitchen equipment arrived in time for the opening. Although waffles were on the breakfast menu, there was no waffle iron. Waitresses were on holiday from college. Service was slow because not all the dishes had arrived, and dish washing was held up by the manual dishwasher who was standing at the sink asking, "Where's the pump?" A couple of years later uniformed waiters bowed to every wish.

*Above:*
*Confederate Jasmine*

*Right:*
*Teeing off on the 18th hole of Harbour Town Links.*
*(Photograph of the Harbour Town Lighthouse is used with permission from Sea Pines Company, Inc.*

# The Marsh Tacky Derby

Early residents were outdoors almost constantly. Their entertainment was beach and water oriented. One such occasion came to pass in 1967 with the First Marsh Tacky Derby - and the last. For almost a century before a bridge and gasoline stations hit the Island, the redoubtable little horse showed its versatility daily in the lives of native farmers. The Marsh Tacky is equally at home behind the plow, pulling a wagon, or cantering under a saddle. No one knows where the name came from, but the late, famous television comedian Garry Moore, who retired here, promoted the following idea in his *Island Packet* column. It went something like this: In a conversation between two Islanders one said to the other, "Where'd you get that tacky horse out standing in the Marsh?"

On a beautiful October day the year of The Marsh Tacky Derby, Islanders met on the beach between the Adventure Inn and the William Hilton Inn. The Arcade supplied hot dogs. Horses were named imaginatively: Cornpone, Hamhock, Hominy, Molasses, and Grits. Why no one continued or has revived this exciting event is as mysterious as the origin of this spunky steed. But then, we were few and so were the rules. For good reasons, no doubt, we can no longer drive cars on the beach, drink a beer or race a horse thereon.

MISS WANDA

# Two Babes and a Boar — A Personal Encounter

Until the early 1970s there was more wildlife on Hilton Head Island than the Marsh Tacky: white-tailed deer, raccoons, a few cougars, and of course the occasional party-goer. My friend Almeda Dow had moved down from New York City and was eager to learn more than how to drive a car and run a washing machine. "I want to know every road and every pig path," she told me.

Little did she realize how prophetic her "pig path" expression would be when I called her to

walk with me in the woods to cut greenery. St. Luke's Episcopal Church was a fledgling mission, and I had been asked to make a large arrangement for Bishop Gray Temple's reception. I chose Perimeter Road to approach the woods because it was near our beach house and I could check on the children's tree house which they had been building in the arms of one of the huge live oaks. Perimeter Road was so named because its sandy ruts curved around the only golf course in that winter of 1964 – Sea Pines Plantation's Ocean Course. (Lawton Villas stand in the road's approximate location. Perimeter Road became Fairway Lane.)

The magnolia leaves were shiny and lush as we entered the woods. We cut and piled our branches

*Alligator, turtle and anhinga catching a few rays.*

quickly. Both Almeda and my cocker spaniel Pepper were eager to go farther into the woods.

"OK," I agreed, "We'll go as far as the children's tree house, and I'll show you their boar rope."

Almeda grabbed my arm to stop me and demanded, "What do you mean 'boar rope'?"

I explained that this had been a favorite Sunday walk for several years for our family and that we always saw wild boar tracks and signs of rooting. One Sunday we had seen three little piglets toddling down the road in front of us. The children wanted to follow them, but their father cautioned that an irate Mama Boar would not be far behind. Exit time.

The Island wild boar, which was last seen here in the 1970s, was really a large pig gone feral, but their snouts and tusks were vicious and the massive breastplate had developed as an armor against poisonous snakes. It was a formidable animal, and snakes were not their *only* enemy.

By the time I had divulged this information to my friend the recent city dweller, her eyes looked like Orphan Annie's.

"What if we see one?" she asked.

"You'll learn how fast you can shinny up the nearest tree. But it's unlikely we'll see anything at high noon other than a squirrel."

Reassured, we continued our walk. Pepper was lost in his world of exquisite smells as we paused to soak the sun in an open place in the woods, feeling content and enjoying the quiet.

The silence was broken by an unmistakable snorting sound. It wasn't Pepper. The snorting came from the distant rear.

I looked behind us and there, about fifty yards down the road, nose to the ground and moving in our direction, was a full-grown wild boar. Only saplings surrounded us, not a single full-grown tree nearby. I touched Almeda's arm, placed my forefinger perpendicular to my lips in the gesture for silence, pointed toward the boar, and pulled her into the middle of a nearby cane patch. Pale though she was, my friend did not panic.

I was certain that the scent of dog was the boar's quarry. I stole a glance down the road just as my little dog burst from the cane patch and darted down the path past the boar. Pepper's four feet scarcely touched the ground as he headed in a zigzag pattern in the direction of home. The boar stopped in his tracks, shook his head, turned, and ran after the dog.

Offering a quick prayer for Pepper, we seized the opportunity he had made possible for us. I touched Almeda's arm again, mouthed the word "Run!" and dashed as fast as my legs would carry me in the opposite direction toward the golf course. Almeda had never mentioned any track trophies, but she passed me like the Tokyo Bullet, knees high and long hair flying. We ran until we could see the 8th fairway on our left and stopped for a congratulatory slap on the back only when we were in the fairway. We desperately wanted to see an animated golf cart. As we trudged toward the golf shop, Almeda didn't see the eight-foot alligator until she fell over it.

While we waited for transportation home, I thought about poor, courageous little Pepper. He had taken on a beast eight times his weight to divert attention from us. There would never be a greater dog.

When we pulled into our driveway, my heart leapt for joy. On the back steps sat Pepper with a triumphant smile on his face. He had won the race.

Almeda and I had double martinis while I fixed Pepper a steak.

"I'll have you know," said our refugee from the canyons of New York, " until today I've never seen anything wilder than a cockroach! From now on, I'm sticking to the beach."

*Right:*
*Bald Eagle*

*Below:*
*Great Egret at sunset*

Raccoon

Great Blue Heron with snake

Speckled Fawn

Three alligators in the Forest Preserve

# Nothing Ventured; Nothing Gained

In the year 2000 Family Circle Tennis moved the tournament to Charleston, and two years later the bankruptcy of MCI WorldCom sent Town and Heritage officials scurrying to find sponsors for the golf tournament which has an estimated $60 million economic impact on this area each year.

As good as everything appeared to be, people trying to make a living on the Island between 1950 and 1975 found it difficult if not impossible. Who knows the numbers who crossed the bridge back to the mainland, down to their last penny, having to start over again elsewhere. Even real estate has not always been good. The first time a Sea Pines Plantation Company salesman sold a lot for $10,000, Charles Fraser came whooping in, called for a celebration, and wondered why anyone would pay that much for a small piece of land. Two years later Greyton Taylor of wine-making fame paid $40,000 for a lot and a half on Beach Lagoon Road, and the rest is wishful reading in a newspaper's real estate section with a few added zeroes. Still, in 1966 it was a gamble to move here.

So was it a gamble when a young orthopedic surgeon from New York docked his boat at Harbour Town and took his first look at Hilton Head Island. Dr. Peter LaMotte decided the Island needed a hospital, and he and a legion of followers set about raising the money and building a superior one, attracting the finest physicians, completing the original building in 1975 when the resident population was 6,500 and the Island had only one traffic light. The first doctor on Hilton Head Island in the mid-1960s had been Chester Goddard who practiced from a small clinic on Pope Avenue. He was followed by Drs. Bill Fries and James Dickensheets.

Prior to that, along with midwives and home remedies, Islanders used the services of young

Bluffton physician Donald Gatch. Dr. Gatch was responsible for making public the embarrassing fact that many native islanders (and other people all over Beaufort County) suffered from intestinal parasites as a result of drinking water from shallow wells. Beaufort County was only beginning to lose its label as a "poverty pocket." The national publicity which followed also pointed to the serious hunger among Beaufort County's less fortunate and was one of the root causes of the Food Stamp legislation being introduced in Congress.

Enter Charlotte Heinrichs, a retired nurse who never actually retired until a few years before her death in 2002. She went to work and single-handedly raised money to provide deep wells, producing healthy domiciles for all Island people. Her Deep Well organization still aids anyone in need of clothing, food, prescriptions or rent money.

We must never forget that Hilton Head had nothing since the turn of the century except its considerable natural beauty. Every building had to be built and it would seem that there has always been the right person to spearhead an enterprise. Again, it is the people who have made all this possible.

*Above:
Four-lane bridge connecting Hilton Head Island to the mainland.*

*Opposite page:
The Haig Point ferry transports guests to Daufuskie Island.*

Those same people have been known to grumble about The Bridge. Somehow each one believes the Island would be a better place if only The Bridge had been closed as soon as each one of them moved here – no matter what year. Not as much is heard about "burning the bridge" since 1973 when the old two-lane James F. Byrnes Crossing was struck by a runaway barge and traffic was suspended for a month while repairs were made. Until the Corps of Engineers completed a pontoon bridge, the local Coast Guard Auxiliary quickly went into action and supplied the Island with daily needs. Local leaders immediately began lobbying for a higher, stationary span with four lanes.

*Painted Bunting. Winters as far south as Panama and arrives on Hilton Head Island annually in late March for half the year.*

*Water Lily*

Wood Duck near cypress tree

Snowy Egrets

# The Last Duck Hunt

Although the Sea Pines Company had already dedicated the 605-acre Forest Preserve as Open Space in a binding covenant, the additional 50 acres in the Audubon Newhall Preserve on Palmetto Bay Road came about in an unusual way.

Before and during the 1960s, hunting was a great sport on Hilton Head Island. Wild turkey, boar, quail, duck – all could be hunted in a single day and the hunter could be lucky in all categories. Shortly before Christmas one year some well-known islanders organized a duck hunt in the open space known as the Sea Pines Forest Preserve. The hunters gathered near an old rice field where cattails made a fine cover for the hunters and a field filled with water a great lure for mallards. The decoys were set and, as the sun came up, the hunters sounded their duck calls.

Ducks came flying in on cue, and the hunters simultaneously blasted away with their shotguns. Blood-curdling screams erupted from nearby bushes and a group of irate men and women, mostly women, came pouring forth led by a very feisty lady, Beanie Newhall. The hunters were certain someone had been hit, but no, this was the first Christmas bird count on the Island and it had been woefully disturbed.

Beanie was at Charles Fraser's office when Fraser arrived. She could state her case quite forcefully, and she pulled out all the stops. By noon Beaufort attorney G. G. Dowling was drawing up papers for the Governor's signature, and shortly thereafter Hilton Head was declared a no-hunting zone and bird sanctuary.

As a peace offering Beanie Newhall was granted 50 acres in perpetuity for a nature preserve.

*Resurrection Fern before the rain*

*Poppies*

Resurrection Fern
after the rain

Swamp or Bog Iris

Giving land became contagious. The Hack family gave land on the "north" end of the Island to the First Presbyterian Church and for a county library to replace the Bookmobile. The Hacks, who owned and lived at Honey Horn Plantation, also offered a simple frame chapel, painted white, for Sunday Protestant services. Itinerant preachers conducted services every Sunday for about 20 people who were grateful for a breeze through the open windows of a church without air conditioning. Cows comprised a welcoming committee and would-be worshippers shooed them away from the gate in the anchor fence surrounding the building. A pianist played the hymns. Sunday school was held in the loft of one of the barns.

On a typically warm December Sunday, the preacher of the week had just read the Christmas Story from the Gospel according to St. Luke. Through the open window at the end of an aisle, a large cow with big, gentle eyes poked her head. All agreed it was truly a Nativity Scene.

This same chapel has been moved to the grounds of the First Presbyterian Church and serves as a place for small weddings and celebrations.

In 1983 the approximately 12,500 residents voted to incorporate the Town of Hilton Head Island as a municipality. Just about everyone has been on a first-name basis with the mayors and much has been accomplished to direct growth. Inspired by the land use covenants of former developers, the Town continues to buy available land for parks and recreational activities along the major arteries. When the Town of Hilton Head bought Honey Horn Plantation, the Council leased the land and buildings to the Museum of Hilton Head.

With development of Palmetto Dunes in late 1960s, followed by Shipyard in 1970 and Hilton Head Plantation in 1971, the first murmurs promoting an alternate route to access the south end of the Island were heard.

Thirty years passed before the Cross Island Parkway was completed in 1997, not a moment too soon for the 30,000 permanent residents and for annual visitors numbering a million and a half.

Here is a case of coming full circle: two hundred years before the completion of the Cross Island Parkway, Beaufort County's shipbuilding industry was one of the largest in the 13 colonies. The deep-water creeks around Hilton Head and the prevalence of hardwoods (like live oak) made the Island a popular place for shipbuilding. The USS Constitution (Old Ironsides) was rebuilt in 1997 using live oaks felled during construction of the Cross Island Parkway.

The Parkway's total cost was $81 million for construction, land acquisition and planning. The original bridge to the Island, the two-lane toll swing bridge, was constructed at a cost of $1.5 million.

*White Ibis rookery.*

*Great Egret fishing.*

*Sanderling and Western Sandpiper*

*Cloud of Royal Terns*

Gull at sunset

*Shore birds feeding: Western Sandpiper, Sanderling, Ruddy Turnstones—
a lesson in the art of camouflage.*

*Above:
Shrimp boat
coming home.*

*Right:
Going out
for the day.*

# In Conclusion

The text of this book has dealt primarily with a period in Hilton Head Island's history since the beginning of the Civil War. The local library, bookstores, and museum have several more detailed books dealing with other Island history. The Port Royal area which includes Hilton Head, since the early sixteenth century, has been under six flags: Spanish, French, English, Scotch, Confederate, and the United States. Although the nomadic Indians had no flag, they were surely on Hilton Head first and left behind many arrow and spear points, shell rings, and some remains of dwellings.

As difficult as it may seem today, originally Hilton Head Island was a hard sell and its first appointed real estate agent, Alexander Trench, failed miserably. The year was 1727 and the Spanish, with headquarters in St. Augustine to the south, were still a threat – as were pirates. Nevertheless, fifty years later, a more intrepid salesman advertised in a Charleston newspaper that he had "healthy and pleasantly located indigo lands" for sale. America was free of war and the King, and the South was poised to embrace a new king, King Cotton. The Elliott family, on land located in what is now Hilton Head Plantation, raised the first successful crop of long-staple cotton that brought wealth and fame to the sea islands, until the day of the "Big Gun Shoot" when the Southern world changed forever.

*The Schooner Welcome glides past Calibogue Cay back to its dock at Shelter Cove Harbour.*

Why, then, has Hilton Head been accorded a different destiny than the other islands strung along the coast of the United States? Why has Hilton Head burst from a quiet but beautiful sea island into a resort and retirement community known in all points of the globe? Charles Fraser, in his 1988 publication, *The Art of Community Building,* cites a "12-cylinder economic engine" as the reason.

- God-Given Natural Beauty
- Transportation Accessibility
- Responsible Private Entrepreneurs
- Effective Mosquito Control
- Adequate Labor Force
- Residential Air Conditioning
- Construction of Basic Infrastructure
- Outstanding Medical Services
- Splendid Volunteer Groups (fostered churches, hospitals, sports, theater, art league)
- Award-winning Architecture
- Best-in-the-world Sports Facilities
- Full-service Beach Hotels

*Photograph of the Harbour Town Lighthouse is used with permission from Sea Pines Company, Inc.*

On a personal note, I have lived on Hilton Head Island since 1961 and today I am constantly asked if I like the Island better now or then? If the question were placed on a balance scale, I think the answer would weigh equally – now *and* then. The conveniences and cultural enlightenment of today can certainly balance the "deserted island" feeling so valuable to the xenophobe. Had we known Hilton Head would become so successful, would the residents have participated in marketing the Island so willingly, would we have proudly told our friends of the great discovery we had made, or would we have kept all these things and pondered them, keeping the Island for ourselves alone? I think we would have taken the course we have taken. What is a wonderful thing if not shared? In sharing, we have asked for help in continuing to make this Island, now that it is almost wholly developed, a haven of happiness, a cooperative venture in the best of all possible worlds.

# Acknowledgements

The danger of acknowledging help in the publication of a book lies in omitting all the little kindnesses and favors done by so many as a book is born. Here are but a few: my daughter Jane Orr and my son Jim Orr for editing and contributions, Major General Howard Davis, the late Charles E. Fraser, Joe Gray, Hilton Head Monthly, The Island Packet's David Lauderdale and Penny Starr, Natalie Hefter of the Coastal Discovery Museum, Friends of the Earth and Brent Blackwelder, Sea Pines Company, Inc., Bob Insley, Frederick Hack, Bill Littell, and Leslie and J.R. Richardson.

# Author

**Margaret Greer's** love affair with Hilton Head Island began in 1961 when she made the island her permanent home. Few people lived among the giant oak trees, and the beaches were relatively free of people except for a few day visitors. No traffic lights existed for there was little traffic on the two lanes of Hwy. 178. In this quiet time Greer began collecting oral history and the few published books on the island's fascinating history.

Along with numerous magazine and newspaper articles on the subjects, she has written books about the island's natural beauty, its architecture, and she is the author of *The Sands of Time: A History of Hilton Head Island.*

# Photograher

A lifetime naturalist specializing in birding, with a life list of over 3,000 species worldwide, **Barry Lowes** (BPHE., M.A.) decided to photograph birds. The quest became his passion and has taken him to all parts of the world photographing birds and animals.

He has earned first-place awards and honorable mentions at the Plantation Wildlife Arts Festival in Thomasville, Georgia, Juried Shows of the Hilton Head Art League, the Southeastern Regional Camera Club's competitions, and The Nature Conservancy. He has been published in brochures, magazines and calendars. His photographs hang in private collections in the USA, Canada, and the UK.

A Canadian from Toronto who winters on Hilton Head Island when not traveling the world, his only wish is that he had begun to photograph seriously earlier in life.

Lowes has a deep concern about the crash of birds, animals and plants which he has witnessed over the 50-plus years he has been a naturalist. He hopes that some of his images will stir viewers to a realization of what is in peril of being lost forever.